T0021282

ASTROLOGY
SELF-CARE

Cancer

ASTROLOGY
SELF-CARE

Cancer

Live your best life
by the stars

Sarah Bartlett

First published in Great Britain in 2022 by Yellow Kite
An imprint of Hodder & Stoughton
An Hachette UK company

1

Illustrations © shutterstock.com

A CIP catalogue record for this title is
available from the British Library

Hardback ISBN 978 1 399 70467 0
eBook ISBN 978 1 399 70468 7
Audiobook ISBN 978 1 399 70469 4

Designed by Goldust Design

Typeset in Nocturne Serif by Hewer Text UK Ltd, Edinburgh
Printed and bound in Great Britain by Clays Ltd, Elcograf S.p.A.

Hodder & Stoughton policy is to use papers that are
natural, renewable and recyclable products and made
from wood grown in sustainable forests. The logging and
manufacturing processes are expected to conform to the
environmental regulations of the country of origin.

Yellow Kite
Hodder & Stoughton Ltd
Carmelite House
50 Victoria Embankment
London EC4Y 0DZ

www.yellowkitebooks.co.uk

'I wonder,' he said, 'whether the stars
are set alight in heaven so that one day
each one of us may find his own again . . .'

Antoine de Saint-Exupéry, French writer

There is a path, hidden between the road of reason and the hedgerow of dreams, which leads to the secret garden of self-knowledge. This book will show you the way.

Contents

Introduction

The ancient Greek goddess Gaia arose from Chaos and was the personification of the Earth and all of Nature. One of the first primordial beings, along with Tartarus (the Underworld), Eros (love) and Nyx (night), as mother of all life, she is both the embodiment of all that this planet is and its spiritual caretaker.

It's hardly likely you will want to become a full-time Mother Earth, but many of us right now are caring more about our beautiful planet and all that lives upon it. To nurture and respect this amazing place we call home, and to preserve this tiny dot in the Universe, the best place to start is, well, with you.

Self-care is about respecting and honouring who you are as an individual. It's about realising that nurturing yourself is neither vanity nor a conceit, but a creative act that brings an awesome sense of awareness and a deeper connection to the Universe and all that's in it. Caring about yourself means you care about everything in the cosmos – because you are part of it.

But self-care isn't just about trekking to the gym, jogging around the park or eating the right foods. It's also about discovering who you are becoming as an individual and caring for that authenticity (and loving and caring about who we are becoming means others can love and care about us, too). This is where the art of sun-sign astrology comes in.

Astrology and Self-Care

So what is astrology? And how can it direct each of us to the right self-care pathway? Put simply, astrology is the study of the planets, sun and moon and their influence on events and people here on Earth. It is an art that has been used for thousands of years to forecast world events, military and political outcomes and, more recently, financial market trends. As such, it is an invaluable tool for understanding our own individuality and how to be true to ourselves. Although there is still dispute within astrological circles as to whether the planets actually physically affect us, there is strong evidence to show that the cycles and patterns they create in the sky have a direct mirroring effect on what happens down here on Earth and, more importantly, on each individual's personality.

Your horoscope or birth-chart is a snapshot of the planets, sun and moon in the sky at the moment you were born. This amazing picture reveals all your innate potential, characteristics and qualities. In fact, it is probably the best 'selfie' you could ever have! Astrology can not only tell you who you are, but also how best to care for that self and your own specific needs and desires as revealed by your birth-chart.

Self-care is simply time to look after yourself – to restore, inspirit and refresh and love your unique self. But it's also about understanding, accepting and being aware of your own traits – both the good and not so good – so that you can then say, 'It's ok to be me, and my intention is to become the best of myself'. In fact, by looking up to the stars and seeing how they reflect us down here on Earth, we can deepen our connection to the Universe for the good of all, too. Understanding that caring about ourselves is not selfish creates an awesome sense of self-acceptance and awareness.

So how does each of us honour the individual 'me' and find the right kind of rituals and practices to suit our personalities? Astrology sorts us out into the zodiac – an imaginary belt encircling the Earth divided into twelve sun signs; so, for example, what one sign finds relaxing, another may find a hassle or stressful. When it comes to physical fitness, adventurous Arians thrive on aerobic work, while soulful Pisceans feel nurtured by yoga. Financial reward or status would inspire the ambitious Capricorn mind, while theatrical Leos need to indulge their joy of being centre stage.

By knowing which sun sign you are and its associated characteristics, you will discover the right self-care routines and practices to suit you. And this unique and empowering book is here to help – with all the rituals and practices in these pages specifically suited to your sun-sign personality for nurturing and vitalising your mind, body and spirit.

However, self-care is not an excuse to be lazy and avoid the goings on in the rest of the world. Self-care is about taking responsibility for our choices and understanding our unique essence, so that we can engage with all aspects of ourselves and the way we interact with the world.

IN A NUTSHELL

Cancer is a sign whose moods, feelings and thoughts flow erratically and are strangely often out of step with the cycle of its ruler, the Moon. Going against the flow of the lunar tides, the Crab fluctuates between the waters of intuition and the realism of dry land. The Crab is hyper-sensitive to their own emotions, as well as the underlying feelings of others. Once they realise they can channel this psychic energy not only into helping others, but also into creating a sense of self-reliance, they can start to care for and live out their Cancer potential.

Sun-Sign Astrology

Also known as your star sign or zodiac sign, your sun sign encompasses the following:

* Your solar identity, or sense of self
* What really matters to you
* Your future intentions
* Your sense of purpose
* Various qualities that manifest through your actions, goals, desires and the personal sense of being 'you'
* Your sense of being 'centred' – whether 'self-centred' (too much ego) or 'self-conscious' (too little ego); in other words, how you perceive who you are as an individual

In fact, the sun tells you how you can 'shine' best to become who you really are.

ASTROLOGY FACTS

The zodiac or sun signs are twelve 30-degree segments that create an imaginary belt around the Earth. The zodiac belt is also known as the ecliptic, which is the apparent path of the sun as it travels round the Earth during the year.

The sun or zodiac signs are further divided into four elements (Fire, Earth, Air and Water, denoting a certain energy ruling each sign), plus three modalities (qualities associated with how we interact with the world; these are known as Cardinal, Fixed and Mutable). So as a Cancerian, for example, you are a 'Cardinal Water' sign.

* Fire signs: Aries, Leo, Sagittarius
  They are: extrovert, passionate, assertive

* Earth signs: Taurus, Virgo, Capricorn
  They are: practical, materialistic, sensual

* Air signs: Gemini, Libra, Aquarius
  They are: communicative, innovative, inquisitive

* Water signs: Cancer, Scorpio, Pisces
  They are: emotional, intuitive, understanding

The modalities are based on their seasonal resonance according to the northern hemisphere.

Cardinal signs instigate and initiate ideas and projects.
They are: Aries, Cancer, Libra and Capricorn

Fixed signs resolutely build and shape ideas.
They are: Taurus, Leo, Scorpio and Aquarius

Mutable signs generate creative change and adapt ideas to reach a conclusion.
They are: Gemini, Virgo, Sagittarius and Pisces

Planetary rulers

Each zodiac sign is assigned a planet, which highlights the qualities of that sign:

Aries is ruled by Mars (fearless)
Taurus is ruled by Venus (indulgent)
Gemini is ruled by Mercury (magical)
Cancer is ruled by the moon (instinctive)
Leo is ruled by the sun (empowering)
Virgo is ruled by Mercury (informative)
Libra is ruled by Venus (compassionate)
Scorpio is ruled by Pluto (passionate)
Sagittarius is ruled by Jupiter (adventurous)
Capricorn is ruled by Saturn (disciplined)
Aquarius is ruled by Uranus (innovative)
Pisces is ruled by Neptune (imaginative)

Opposite Signs

Signs oppose one another across the zodiac (i.e. those that are 180 degrees away from each other) – for example, Aries opposes Libra and Taurus opposes Scorpio. We often find ourselves mysteriously attracted to our opposite signs in romantic relationships, and while the signs' traits appear to clash in this 'polarity', the essence of each is contained in the other (note, they have the same modality). Gaining insight into the characteristics of your opposite sign (which are, essentially, inherent in you) can deepen your understanding of the energetic interplay of the horoscope.

On The Cusp

Some of us are born 'on the cusp' of two signs – in other words, the day or time when the sun moved from one zodiac sign to another. If you were born at the end or beginning of the dates usually given in horoscope pages (the sun's move through one sign usually lasts approximately four weeks), you can check which sign you are by contacting a reputable astrologer (or astrology site) (see Resources, p. 115) who will calculate it exactly for you. For example, 23 August is the standardised changeover day for the sun to move into Virgo and out of Leo. But every year, the time and even sometimes the day the sun changes sign can differ. So, say you were born on 23 August at five in the morning and the sun didn't move into Virgo until five in the afternoon on that day, you would be a Leo, not a Virgo.

How To Use This Book

The book is divided into three parts, each guiding you in applying self-care to different areas of your life:

* Part One: your mind and feelings
* Part Two: your body
* Part Three: your soul

Caring about the mind using rituals or ideas tailored to your sign shows you ways to unlock stress, restore focus or widen your perception. Applying the practices in Part One will connect you to your feelings and help you to acknowledge and become aware of why your emotions are as they are and how to deal with them. This sort of emotional self-care will set you up to deal with your relationships better, enhance all forms of communication and ensure you know exactly how to ask for what you want or need, and be true to your deepest desires.

A WORD ON CHAKRAS

Eastern spiritual traditions maintain that universal energy, known as 'prana' in India and 'chi' in Chinese philosophy, flows through the body, linked by seven subtle energy centres known as chakras (Sanskrit for 'wheel'). These energies are believed to revolve or spiral around and through our bodies, vibrating at different frequencies (corresponding to seven colours of the light spectrum) in an upward, vertical direction. Specific crystals are placed on the chakras to heal, harmonise, stimulate or subdue the chakras if imbalance is found.

The seven chakras are:
* The base or root (found at the base of the spine)
* The sacral (mid-belly)
* The solar plexus (between belly and chest)
* The heart (centre of chest)
* The throat (throat)
* The third eye (between the eyebrows)
* The crown (top of the head)

On p. 95 we will look in more detail at how Cancerians can work with chakras for self-care.

Fitness and caring for the body are different for all of us, too. While Cancerians benefit from swimming, Sagittarians prefer to go for a run, and Geminis a daily quick stretch or yoga. Delve into Part Two whenever you're in need of physical restoration or a sensual makeover tailored to your sign.

Spiritual self-care opens you to your sacred self or soul. Which is why Part Three looks at how you can nurture your soul according to your astrological sun sign. It shows you how to connect to and care for your spirituality in simple ways, such as being at one with Nature or just enjoying the world around you. It will show you how to be more positive about who you are and honour your connection to the Universe. In fact, all the rituals and practices in this section will bring you joyful relating, harmonious living and a true sense of happiness.

The Key

Remember, your birth-chart or horoscope is like the key to a treasure chest containing the most precious jewels that make you you. Learn about them, and care for them well. Use this book to polish, nurture, respect and give value to the beautiful gemstones of who you are, and, in doing so, bring your potential to life. It's your right to be true to who you are, just by virtue of being born on this planet, and therefore being a child of Mother Earth and the cosmos.

Care for you, and you care for the Universe.

CANCER
WORDS OF WISDOM

As you embark on your self-care journey, it's important to look at the lunar cycles and specific astrological moments throughout the year. At those times (and, indeed, at any time you choose), the words of Cancer wisdom below will be invaluable, empowering you with positive energy. Taking a few mindful moments at each of the four major phases of every lunar cycle and at the two important astrological moments in your solar year (see Glossary, p. 117) will affirm and enhance your positive attitude towards caring about yourself and the world.

NEW CRESCENT MOON – to care for yourself:

'I honour my soft, gentle, kind nature and know it is mine, and mine alone.'

'I must learn to nourish myself first, others second.'

'My roots are strong, and I have a deep sense of belonging to myself.'

FULL MOON – for sealing your intention to care for your feeling world:

'I will always remind myself how important my intuition is to me.'

'My compassion is infinite and that includes towards myself.'

'I must experience what it is to live without neediness, but with self-assurance.'

WANING MOON for letting go, and letting things be:

'I will no longer prevaricate but start to act on my values.'

'Time to let go of fear; a risk can be liberating.'

'I will no longer be led by what other people think is right for me.'

DARK OF THE MOON – to acknowledge your 'shadow' side:

'I will become more aware of my indirect approach to confrontation and try to face truth rather than avoid it.'

'I acknowledge that I need to learn to give and take without keeping score.'

'I will no longer sacrifice my true desires for the love of others.'

SOLAR RETURN SALUTATION – welcoming your new solar year to be true to who you are:

Repeat on your birthday: 'I must learn to assert myself openly. This way I will become more comfortable with change, and the dynamic flow of life and love.'

SUN IN OPPOSITION – learn to be open to the opposite perspective that lies within you:

Repeat when the sun is in Capricorn: 'My opposite sign is Capricorn – one of determination, will-power and pragmatism. These attributes are in my birth-chart, too, and this strong sense of purpose and appetite for life is mine to nurture for personal fulfilment.'

The Cancer Personality

Why should we build our happiness on the opinions of others, when we can find it in our own hearts?
Jean-Jacques Rousseau, Swiss philosopher

Characteristics. Caring, emotional, imaginative, intuitive, sensitive, sensual, indirect, nostalgic, subtle, moody, unpredictable, introspective, tenacious, dreamy, self-concerned, evasive, overprotective, secretive, creative, psychic

Symbol: the Crab
In Greek mythology Cancer (Latin for 'crab') is identified with the crab that attacked Heracles while he fought the many-headed Hydra. The crab grabbed Heracles by the foot with his pincers, then Heracles killed him. For his courageous interference in the battle, the goddess Hera placed the crab among the stars as the constellation Cancer.

Planetary ruler: the Moon

The Moon is the Earth's only natural satellite and is the main gravitational influence on the tides. The side of the Moon nearest to the Earth is marked by dark volcanic 'maria' or 'seas' (ancient pools of solidified lava) that fill the spaces between rocky highlands and vast craters. The Moon's phases, cycles and eclipses, and its powerful presence in our sky, have had a profound influence on all forms of culture, mythology, belief systems and calendars throughout global history.

Astrological Moon: Depending on which zodiac sign the Moon is in at the moment of birth, not forgetting its angles and aspects in relation to the other planets, it describes our sense of belonging, our moods, feelings, instincts and how we relate to our birth mother, our sense of mothering (whatever gender we are) and/or the mother archetype within ourselves.

Element: Water

Like Scorpio and Pisces, Cancer is a 'feeling' sign. In other words, to the Water signs, what they actually feel is what is real. They are subjective and soulful, and decisions are made based on gut instinct and emotional understanding. Water signs have an intuitive sense of how to flow with the undercurrents of others.

Modality: Cardinal

Cardinal signs prefer beginning creative projects and are motivated self-starters, keen to take control and achieve results. They are often frustrated if life isn't filled with fresh and new experiences.

Crystal: Moonstone

Body: Breasts, digestive system

Sun-sign profile: The enigmatic, warm-hearted and caring Crab is a bundle of paradoxes. Deep down, Cancerians are the bonding, needy type, yet they also want their independence. They appear coolly self-contained, but are passionate, wild and uninhibited. The Crab wants to belong to someone, yet they hate being possessed. They resist change yet feel pulled in many directions and often find it impossible to commit to anything. As both the lunar carer of the zodiac and also embodying the wilder aspects of moon goddesses such as Artemis and Selene, Cancerians live and breathe a truly 'feminine mystique'. Once this mystical quality is lived out and expressed, rather than denied or internalised, they can begin to love themselves, truly and deeply, living less in fear of what might be, and more in joy of what is right now.

Your best-kept secret: Deep down inside, you feel all the world's feelings, whether pain, desire or laughter. This potential for helping everyone else is about helping yourself, too.

What gives you meaning and purpose in life? A sense of belonging, caring for others, making sure everyone else is happy

What makes you feel good to be you? Financial security, privacy, creativity, visiting historical places, daydreaming, good memories, retreating from the world one day, then engaging fully in it the next

What or who do you identify with? Mothers, family life, chefs and restaurateurs, the place you were born, the sea, healers, female friends, independent people, romantics, head-hunters, entrepreneurs

What stresses you out? A messed-up kitchen, taking risks, not being in control, rejection, the unknown, the future, conflict, taking on too many people's problems, feeling unwanted

What relaxes you? Cooking, nostalgic films, being at home, family get-togethers, interior design, looking through old photos, gazing at the sea or walking along a beach

What challenges you? Finding time to nurture your own dreams and desires; accepting you can't help everyone; learning to help yourself first; finding out your true motives and values

What Does Self-Care Mean For Cancer?

The giving and caring Crab looks after everyone around them, while taking time to care about themselves may seem a lot like selfishness. When it comes to the people they love, the Crab is the most generous, protective and giving of signs. But Cancerians have a hard time accepting self-care is their right. Although they may avidly follow health and beauty tips, join in fitness groups or sign up to a yoga class, they often give up on all their good intentions. Fearing commitment, it's the old cry of, 'Well I may go to the gym later, but I'm not sure I want to be there at the same time every day'. If a Cancerian sets their own self-care goals at their own pace, whether erratic or not, what matters is that self-care becomes a dynamic joy, not just a feeling of they 'must do' this or that when they're expected to. You may already 'do' a load of self-care stuff to set a good example to your family, or to feel loved and admired by your peers or a group you've joined. But are you doing it for you?

Self-Care Focus

For kindly Cancerians, self-care is more than just fitness and nutrition. It's embracing their creativity, channelling their psychic sensitivity, understanding the mystique of their Cancer myth and cherishing the mother and the wild woman within, all the while not forgetting their continued support for their loved ones. Most of all, it's about realising the Crab's need to tap into their deepest roots – their heritage and their past – and understanding not only their relationship with their 'birth mother,' whether a loving or fearsome one, but also how they live out their own mothering instinct. So in that sense, Cancerians need to find a feeling of belonging, not to just their family, clan or friends, but also deep within themselves.

This book will delight you with the kind of care that brings out the best of you, so you can truly find happiness and joy in life, as well as the realisation that you can find your authentic self and embark on the wonderful journey to belonging to you, and who you are becoming.

PART ONE

Caring For Your Mind And Feelings

The most painful thing is losing yourself in the process of loving someone too much and forgetting that you are special, too.

Ernest Hemingway, American novelist

This section will inspire you to delight in your thoughts, express your ideas and take pleasure in your feelings. Once you get that deep sense of awareness of who you are and what you need, not only will it feel good to be alive, but you will be even more content to be yourself. The rituals and practices here will boost your self-esteem, motivate you to lead a more serene existence and enhance all forms of relationships with others. The most important relationship of all, with yourself, will be nurtured in the best possible way according to your sun sign.

Like the other Water signs, Scorpio and Pisces, the Cancer mind is informed by their feeling and intuitive world, in that 'if it feels right, then I'll do it'. The practices in this section will enhance Cancerians' intuitive powers and provide the confidence to live out the desires and intentions that fill their minds.

The great well of emotion that rises from the watery depths within the Crab means you have the power to heal both others and yourself. Here, you will discover ways to channel that sensibility, and to see how to use it positively to care for you. Every Cancerian, ruled by the moon, also needs to let the moonlight shine into their world. Aligning with the lunar cycles will help you not only achieve your goals, but also engage at the 'right time', whether for self-confidence, chilling out or just tuning into your creative mindset. Here, you can learn the importance of putting your own needs first, rather than living vicariously through others, and discover a true sense of self-worth.

It is time to 'mother' yourself first and foremost, so that if you want to be the best carer in town, you're off to a polished, dedicated and authentic start.

ALIGNING TO THE LUNAR CYCLE

✳

According to astrological lore, all zodiac signs are influenced by the moon's cycle in some way or another. Ruled by the moon, however, Cancer is thought to be affected by its changing energy more than any other sign. Cancerians' moodiness is said to reflect this but it is often not in harmony with the lunar phases. Rather than move out on to the creative tide when the moon is waxing or on to the beach of efficiency at the full moon, you scuttle into your shell, and miss the moon's beneficial energy. So instead of being the Crab who prevaricates, here's how to make use of the four main phases of lunar energy in your life, to invoke a happier mindset and flow more easily between the demands of everyday life (let's call that dry land) and a deeper acceptance and understanding of your feeling world (the ocean).

You will need:
* A bowl
* 4 moonstones
* 4 white candles
* 4 silver rings

Keep the rings and stones together in a box, until you need them, and read on for the four parts of this moon-cycle practice (each of which requires different combinations of ingredients).

Waxing moon for creating a mindful pathway
When the moon is waxing, between new and full, this is the time to start new projects, focus on creative ideas and begin your new self-care routine (whether a fitness-based programme or the rituals in this book – starting with this one!). Once you are in harmony with the lunar energy, you will become more aware of your intentions, desires and needs. Perform this simple ritual during the waxing phase to open yourself to this flow of energy.

1. On an evening of a waxing moon, fill the bowl of water and place it on a table.

2. Light the candles and place them around the bowl.

3. Place one moonstone and a silver ring in the bowl.

4. Say, 'With the waxing moon, inspiration, creativity and intentions can now be set for my future goals'.

5. Blow out the candles when you feel you are ready – perhaps when you have focused and felt a sense of peace, gazing into the water or the candle flame for a few minutes.

6. Leave the bowl overnight.

In the morning, you will feel aligned to the lunar energy, ready to adapt, go with the flow and follow your instincts towards achieving a goal.

Full moon for fulfilling a project or idea

Now, some Crabs are aware of the full moon phase – it may influence their moods and habits, make them emotional, indecisive, acutely sensitive to the world around them. But that's not much help to you, unless you learn to work positively with it to maximise its powerful energy. Full moons are for completing a project, for the culmination and implementation of an idea and for closing a deal or making a commitment. This ritual will remind you to do all of these, including committing to caring about who you are becoming.

1. On the evening of the full moon, take your bowl of water, and this time place in it two moonstones and two rings.

2. Surround the bowl with the four candles and light them.

3. Say: 'I will not give in to my negative thoughts. Deep down I can see the way forward and will now make a commitment to my desire.'

4. As above, blow out the candles when you feel you are ready, and leave the bowl overnight.

In the morning, you will be ready to commit yourself and move forwards.

Waning moon for review, reflection and certainty
This is the time to reflect on what your intentions were during the waxing-moon phase and how you can now review your full-moon commitment to help you in the future.

1. During an evening of a waning moon, place three moonstones and three rings in the bowl of water.

2. Light the four candles, and say, 'I can now put into practice all the plans I have made during the waxing moon and will be true to the promise I made to myself under the full moon'.

3. Again, blow out the candles when you are ready and leave overnight.

In the morning, you will begin to notice that your self-care intentions will soon be made manifest.

Dark of the moon for revival

Finally, the dark-of-the-moon phase (when the moon is invisible) is the time to revive, dream and open yourself to your intuition, so you can be ready for the beginning of the next lunar cycle.

1. Place four moonstones and four rings into the bowl of water.

2. Light the candles and say, 'I am now ready to rest, reflect and dream a while, to restore my energy and flow with the moon, ready for the next cycle'.

3. Once you have blown out the candles, leave overnight.

In the morning you will be more aware of how restorative this phase of the moon is and how it will help you to clarify your self-care goals.

Using the four rituals above for at least three or four lunar cycles, you will begin to feel aligned with the fluctuating energy of the moon and, by learning to flow with it, know that you are, at last, acting in the best possible way to achieve Cancer's self-care goals at the most auspicious times.

SELF-ESTEEM SHRINE

♡

It's only natural for Cancerians to want to protect and nurture other people, but by doing so, you lose touch with your own personal power and talents. Here's a way to ground and balance this energy, so restoring and boosting your own self-value. Shield others, yes – love them for being who they are, come to their aid when they ask you and be there for them – but first, belong only to yourself.

A shrine is simply a place where we honour or pay respect to someone or something. Here, you can pay homage to yourself at any time of day to uplift your spirit and restore self-belief.

You will need:
* A shelf or small table that won't be disturbed
* Two pink candles
* A small mirror to prop up behind the shrine
* A piece of rose-quartz crystal
* A moonstone
* A choice souvenir, object or photo that means something to you

1. On your shelf or small table, place the candles in front of the mirror and light them.

49

2. Place a stone beside each candle, and your souvenir or memorabilia wherever you feel is right for you.

3. Sit quietly for a moment to find stillness, then say the following affirmations as you gaze at yourself in the mirror:

I am always here to help friend or family, but now I am here to help myself.

I am grateful for the support of others and for my feelings and how they can guide me to know the truth.

I honour my true purpose.

I honour my past, present and future.

I acknowledge my self-worth and my potential for being true to that self.

4. Blow out the candles.

Go to this place, your shrine, whenever you need to be reminded of your personal power, your awesome self, your belief in your desires and intentions, and be uplifted by the lunar glow that shines through you.

HAPPY FAMILIES

♡

There are two kinds of Cancer relationships with family and the past; the first is empowering and supportive, the second is needy and dependent. Here's how to renounce the latter.

Cancerians have a strong empathy with the past, both their own and in history books. This gives them a sense of continuity and, therefore, security. A family tree is something you can't change – it's a fixed pattern of what has been in your past – and so enables Cancerians to feel contained and that they belong. So create and use the 'family tree' below – a family made up of all that is good within you – to feel a sense of that continuity you are looking for and promote happy days.

You will need:

* A pen
* A drawing, painting or image of a branching tree that you like, about A4 size
* 9 (the number of continuity, completion and new beginnings) cut-out images of leaves (or leaf-shaped scraps of paper), coloured in
* Glue or sticky tape

1. Write on each 'leaf' a word to sum up what makes you happy. It could be a physical exercise, a friend, an emotion, a thought. Maybe, 'gardening', 'cooking' or 'love'. You have nine 'happy families' to consider, so don't rush – take your time.

2. When you have written your nine happy words, stick them on your tree, in any arrangement you like, then say: 'My happy family is within me and grows like the branches of this tree. I will enjoy all these qualities and desires, and create my own heritage, as I experience each one, time and time again.'

You can add more leaves, remove or cover others with new ones and, as you become more creative with your Cancer family tree and care for it more, you will feel a sense of caring and belonging to the family within yourself.

SELF-BELIEF PRACTICE

The Crab finds a sense of integrity and self-confidence when they feel something is right, or their intuition leads them to some form of personal achievement. But if things don't go according to those gut instincts, they will feel inadequate.

Perform this ritual on a waxing-moon evening.

You will need:
* A white tea light
* A piece of clear quartz

1. Light your candle.

2. Hold your piece of clear quartz and turn it around and around in your hands, while you say the following:

I restore self-belief and, with it, self-love.
I restore self-love and the love of others.
With love, I restore belonging to myself.
Belonging to myself, I have self-belief.

3. Place the quartz before the candle and let the candle burn down for a minute or so to invoke the energy of self-love and self-belief around you.

4. When you feel you are ready – perhaps after you have gazed into the candle flame for a few minutes – blow out the candle to seal your intention.

Practising this ritual will free you from self-doubt, renew self-esteem and restore self-belief and, with it, self-love.

LETTING GO

✳

The Crab has a propensity, claw-like, to hang on tightly to anything that gives them a sense of security. They quickly form attachments to people, things, places, memories, regrets, even grudges, 'what-ifs' and romantic illusions. Mother's apron strings and umbilical cords aside, this need for bonding is both a blessing and a curse. The blessing is that you have the gift of love to form bonds with people through your care; but you also need to learn to loosen the knots a little, so that you can be more independent.

The symbolic 'untying of knots' here means you can fearlessly take the next step and find your own time and space to build the security needed within you to nurture your secret dreams.

You will need:
* A white candle
* A selenite wand (or pointed piece of selenite)
* A 60cm (24 inch) length of silver ribbon, along which you have made four equidistant knots

1. Place the candle on a table.

2. Hold the selenite in one hand and the length of ribbon or twine in the other.

3. Facing north, turn around in an anticlockwise direction, drawing an invisible magic circle of protection around yourself, using the point the crystal, and say:
>   Here I let go of the past and all that is bound,
>   Bring me grace, forgiveness and all that is found.
>   I now start afresh, and follow the path,
>   Fearless and certain of where I can start.

4. Wind the knotted ribbon around the crystal and place it on the ground. Now say:
>   The knots untied free me from chains.
>   The knots untied restore my flame.
>   The knots untied release my fear.
>   The knots untied restore my cheer.

5. Finally, pick up the ribbon and untie each knot, repeating a line of the verse above for each knot untied.

6. Light the candle to seal your intention to free yourself from the 'ties' that bind you. Reflect on your future pathway and the promise you have made to yourself for a happy future free from the wrong kind of attachments.

This practice will help you to replace the fear of letting go with a fearless step forward on your journey to honouring your integrity.

....

OUT WITH OVERTHINKING

♡

Even though Cancer is motivated by the spontaneous feelings of 'if it's good to go, I'll do it', once engaged in any new objective, overthinking may put you off course. Here's a way to unload any worrying niggles of negativity that may overcome you.

You will need:
* A mirror
* A paper and pen
* A handful of coffee beans or scraps of paper
* A paper bag

1. Look at yourself in the mirror.

2. Write a list of the things you don't like about yourself – not necessarily things you see in the mirror. Be creative with this – for example, if you don't like your voice, transform it into a practical and positive expression of that quality, manifesting your thoughts in the tangible written word; so you could write, 'I'm going to start loving my unique voice' or 'I'm going to become a great singer'. If you don't like your laziness, or hate getting up in the morning, say, 'I'm going to get up in the morning and smile at the day, for every day is a gift'.

3. Face the mirror again, look yourself straight in the eye and say aloud what your fears or vulnerabilities are. We all have them, so don't deceive yourself that you don't – that's a belief system you'll need to dump straight away.

4. Write down on the piece of paper the list of fears, inadequacies or any other current issues you have.

5. Once you have two lists, count out the coffee beans or scraps of paper – one for each of the issues you have listed. These represent the stuff that you don't like and don't accept in your life, and you're not going to think about any more. Because every time you think 'doubt' or 'fear' or 'no one understands me', you will simply get doubt, fear and misunderstanding thrown back at you.

6. Put the beans or scraps in the paper bag, close your eyes, then gradually remove them, one by one, and place them on your written testaments. As you remove each one, affirm to yourself: 'I deserve to love and care about myself just by virtue of being on this planet'.

7. When you have finished, carefully crumple up your written statements and chuck them in the rubbish bin, along with the beans or scraps.

You are now free to take the next step towards self-love. If you do get negative thoughts overwhelming your mind, simply repeat the affirmation in step 6 over and over again for a few minutes to remind yourself of how you have dumped your self-reproaching way of thinking.

THE TRIPLE GODDESS LUNAR CHARM

★★
★

For Cancerians, there's often a twinge of guilt attached to self-care, as if people are going to judge or condemn them. Here's a ritual to help release yourself from this self-conscious emotion and replace it with an enjoyment in caring about you.

In lunar lore, there are three aspects of the divine feminine – archetypes known as the maiden, the mother and the crone. Appearing in neopagan tradition, the maiden (waxing moon) symbolises creativity, the mother (full moon) represents fertility and the crone (waning moon) symbolises wisdom. The symbol of the triple goddess is two crescent moons flanking a full moon.

This ritual will connect you to the joy of caring about these Cancerian potentials.

You will need:

* A white candle
* An image of the triple goddess symbol
* A piece of paper and a pen
* 3 moonstones or clear quartz crystals

1. On the evening of a new crescent or waxing-moon phase, light the candle for atmosphere.

2. Draw the image of the triple goddess on your piece of paper.

3. Place the three crystals on each of the motifs of the phases of the moon.

4. Take up the first crystal to the left and blow gently on to it, to connect your breath to its power. Replace the crystal.

5. Leave your petition in place until the evening of the full moon, then pick up the central crystal and repeat as above.

6. Again, leave until the waning-moon phase and take up the third crystal and repeat.

7. Now leave until the next new crescent moon, then take up the three crystals and put them in a safe place to enhance all forms of self-empowerment, wisdom and fulfilment.

Use this symbolism to align yourself to the energies of the Cancer moon, to promote a sense of universal creative joy and also to empower and uplift yourself. Then truly caring about you is no longer a guilt trip but a blessing.

Relationships

As a natural carer for others, the Crab finds it easy to relate to family, friends and colleagues, as long as they can lend a helping hand or offer some form of advice. Yet because of their changing moods, they find it hard to commit themselves to specific dates and can infuriate their loved ones with their erratic behaviour.

Romantically, Cancerians are rarely direct about their desires or needs and take ages to let a potential admirer know they're even a little bit interested. Passively seductive, the Crab makes sure that they're not going to be fooled or deceived and looks for complete trust and security before they'll commit themselves to anything more than a few dates. The compassionate Crab often also falls for needy or lonely people, simply because human weakness and vulnerability pluck at their own soft heartstrings. Once in a relationship, though, the Crab loves to be needed and will do anything for the love of their life. That said, they are renowned for swinging between clinginess and coldness, an ambivalence reflecting both their need for constant reassurance and their fear of rejection.

Once Cancerians commit, they usually do so for ever (even if they regret their decision further down the line);

they not only have a great nesting instinct but will care for and create a strong family support system around their relationship.

....

LOVE MYSELF

*

Being cool and aloof on the surface, the Cancerian often sends out unconscious signals to would-be lovers that although they may be the iconic caretakers of everyone's needs, they don't always want to be smothered with love themselves. Perform this ritual every full moon to affirm that you're open to be loved by others, and also by yourself.

You will need:
* A piece of A4 paper and a pen/pencil
* 4 pink tea lights
* 4 pieces of rose-quartz crystal

1. On the piece of paper draw a rough heart shape to fill the page.

2. Place one candle at the top, one at the bottom, one to the left and one to the right of the shape.

3. Place a piece of rose quartz beside each candle.

4. Light the candles and then pick up the rose-quartz pieces, one at a time, then replace them, each time saying: 'I am open to love, I deserve love, I am loved by myself and others'.

5. Blow out the candles and leave the crystal petition until the next waxing moon to welcome the love that is due to you.

A true sense of self-worth and confidence will replace any Cancerian doubt or overthinking about how loveable you really are.

....

ATTRACTING ROMANCE

✳

When looking for love, the Crab often hesitates or puts off making a decision, then misses out on a new romantic opportunity for fear of making a wrong choice. To ensure you invite the 'right kind of romance', so you no longer have to play the 'will-I-or-won't-I' game, perform this simple ritual during a waxing-moon phase.

You will need:
* A red candle
* A white candle
* A pink candle
* A rose-quartz crystal
* A bowl of water
* A silver spoon (coloured or real)

1. Place the three candles in a triangle with the red at the top (the object of your desire), the white at the bottom left (your lunar personality) and the pink at the bottom right (your romantic ideal).

2. Light the candles, and in front of you place the rose quartz in the bowl of water.

3. Stir the surface of the water with the silver spoon in a clockwise direction, as if you were stirring love and desire into someone's heart. As you do so say: 'I will find love by aligning to the moon's power to protect and guide me in romance'.

4. Once the water has stopped swirling, remove the rose-quartz crystal, blow out the candles and keep the crystal with you until the full moon.

This practice will invoke and attract trust in new romance coming into your life.

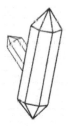

....

SOLSTICE LOVE

✳

The sign of Cancer corresponds to the summer solstice in the northern hemisphere, which has long been associated with celebrating the sun as it reaches its zenith or highest point in the sky. The summer solstice represents the fulfilment of love, commitment, completion of a project, beneficial changes for the future and self-empowerment.

As you are a natural-born child of the summer solstice, you are blessed with the power to practise this ritual any time of year to enhance your giving, loving nature and to show that your love is the most caring, restorative and sincerest of all, both for others and yourself.

You will need:
* A candle
* An image of a pentagram (5-pointed star)
* A piece of paper and pen
* 5 pieces of selenite or moonstone

1. On the evening of a full moon (this corresponds to the same energy as the summer solstice), light your candle for atmosphere and find stillness. For a few moments, focus on the flame and recall all the things you love about life, yourself and others.

2. Copy the pentagram shape on to your piece of paper, with one point facing north to align you with solstice energy.

3. Write your name in the centre of the star and place a crystal within each of the drawn points.

4. Now say this affirmation to confirm love for others and self: 'With this ritual pentagram, the solar light brings me grace, renews self-esteem, enhances love and brings me the joy of becoming true to the lunar child that I am – nurturing, wild and free'.

Perform this ritual whenever you need a boost of self-love and to genuinely spread that love among family, friends and the world.

PART TWO

Caring For Your Body

If anything is sacred, the
human body is sacred.

Walt Whitman, American poet

Here, you will discover alternative ways to look after and nurture your body, not just as a physical presence, but its connection to mind and spirit, too. This section gives you a wide range of ideas, from using sun-sign crystals to protect your physical and psychic self to fitness, diet and beauty tips. There are specific chakra practices and yoga poses especially suited to your sun sign, not forgetting bath-time rituals and calming practices to destress you and nurture holistic wellbeing.

Cancerian moods, energy levels and metabolism, not forgetting eating habits and beauty routines, fluctuate erratically. The Crab goes through periods of trying out new fitness programmes suggested by their friends, but often gives up when it all gets too demanding on their time. But saying 'yes' to please others means you're not actually pleasing yourself, when you really know deep down inside what you want to do. For example, if you feel like reading a book and your friend wants you to play tennis, well, gently thank them for the offer, refuse and read the book. You'll feel better for saying 'no', rather than resentfully finding yourself stuck on court in a game of tennis that doesn't interest you.

By acknowledging and accepting that you need to go it alone in your own time, you can plan your bodily health strategies accordingly, and even take advantage of the moon's waxing and waning energy. This will vitalise and restore you, bringing you physical health, with a sense of holistic harmony too.

Fitness and Movement

The last thing independent Cancer needs is to become dependent on a routine set by others. It may sound good on paper to get down to the latest dance class or join a jogging group around the park, but frankly, when it comes to keeping fit, the Crab does it best on their own, in their own time and usually from home, where they feel safe, secure and not beholden to the demands of others.

CORE STRENGTH

♡

With a need to ground your emotional energy into something solid and tangible, the best exercises are those which work your core (where your instinctive, emotional nature is rooted) such as Pilates and yoga. If you feel centred and nurtured in your core, this enables you to stay strong when you're running around nurturing everyone else. Don't disregard the power of water either, as it helps to calm and support your nervous system. Swim, run on the beach, sail, windsurf or just paddle your feet in the surf – anything water-related will benefit your Water-sign energy.

WORKING THE BODY

♡

Your core is made up of various different muscles – your abs and obliques, as well as your glutes and back muscles. All these need to be worked and trained to strengthen the centre of your body, which is so important for overall Cancer fitness.

Start off with 'side plank' to target your obliques, then complete your session with 'whole body reviver' – a low-impact core move that helps improve overall stability.

Side plank

1. Lying on your left side, bring your left elbow directly under your left shoulder. Place your top foot on top or in front of your bottom foot.

2. Push your hips upwards to raise up your body, and straighten your supporting arm, keeping your core and lower shoulder muscles engaged.

3. Raise your right arm above your head and stretch it up as far as you can.

4. Hold for a count of 10 breaths, while focusing on your breathing.

Whole body reviver

1. Position yourself on all fours, with your knees under your hips and your hands under your shoulders. Remember to keep your back flat and long.

2. Reach out in front of you with your right hand and extend your left leg out behind you.

3. Round your back and bend your head down; connect your right elbow to your left knee.

4. Return your arm and leg to their extended positions and repeat this movement in time with your breathing for 10 counts.

5. Repeat on the other side.

Both of these exercises can be done before or after any yoga or Pilates session to tone, stabilise and energise your physical centre of gravity, and Cancer's emotional equilibrium, too.

BEACH EXERCISE

♡

Not every Cancerian can live or be by the sea, but if you can, take advantage of this, your most natural, symbolic icon of lunar power (the sea as nurturer, cleanser and unforgiving in her wild aspect) and run beside the surf. If you can't get down to a beach, then just imagine the sea beside you or listen to the surf through headphones as you do this simple, beneficial exercise.

1. Start to gently jog along the beach (or wherever you are with the sound of the surf in your ears) and take a steady rhythm, breathing in time with your steps.

2. Imagine the tide coming in as you breathe in, and out as you breathe out. Feel how the in-breath is filling you with tidal power, then releasing all your negative energy as you breathe out.

Each time you breathe in, you are restored and nourished by the moon; each time you breathe out you are cleansed and ready to be replenished. After you have jogged for about ten minutes, you'll not only feel physically empowered, but also emotionally restored.

....

YOGA POSES

♡

There are two yoga poses that will nurture the Cancerian core and digestive system, while bringing balance to the extremes of lunar energy. The supine spinal twist is empowering, while the child's pose brings calm and stillness. Whether you're new to yoga or are already practising, perform these two poses whenever you feel in the mood.

Child's pose

1. Kneel on a mat and separate your knees as wide as the mat, with toes still touching.

2. Bring your belly to rest between your thighs and gently place your forehead to the floor. Relax the shoulders, jaw and eyes. (The energy point at the centre of the forehead stimulates the vagus nerve – responsible for the regulation of internal organ functions, such as digestion, heart rate and respiratory rate, among other things – and soothes the whole nervous system.)

3. Stretch your arms out in front of you with palms towards the floor, and the fingers of both hands touching each other.

4. Stay in this pose for a few minutes or so, to bring stillness, peace and calm.

Spinal twist
1. Lie on your back with both legs straight in front of you.

2. Bend your right knee and draw it into your chest, then drape it across your body, towards the floor on the left. If you can touch the floor with your knee, so much the better for this twist.

3. Extend both arms into a T position (perpendicular to the body) and turn your head to the right. (You can also reach out with your left hand to touch your right knee.)

4. Close your eyes and stay for about 10–15 breaths, and then return to the starting position.

5. Now switch sides.

To replenish and balance your emotional energy levels, perform these poses at the new-moon and full-moon phases.

Nutrition

The stomach, digestive system, breasts and womb are all associated with Cancer. To maintain good health in all these areas, consider reducing caffeine and add supplements or foods rich in potassium to help with fluid balance (whether water retention or fluctuating weight issues), not forgetting being more aware of your eating habits.

Cancerians often eat for comfort, and emotional eating leads to overindulgence. Of course, enjoy the good things in life, and it's great to feel nurtured by food and the joy of cooking, but don't use food as the answer to your worries or inhibitions. Lovingly prepare food that you know is healthy, and with awareness of what you're eating. Perhaps make a conscious note of which foods you turn to when your moods are up or down? Allow yourself to indulge in a guilty pleasure one day a week; otherwise, stick to a well-balanced diet and you will feel more comfortable with yourself and more in tune with your changeable nature.

WEIGHT MAINTENANCE

★★
★

The fluctuations in Cancerians' weight depend not just on the time of the month, or even the year, but also on those changing eating patterns. This simple ritual will set you on course for sticking to your eating goals. You can't change your weight by magic, but you can use this to put you on track for maintaining that balance.

You will need:

- A piece of clear quartz crystal
- A mirror
- Lavender essential oil
- Paper and pen

1. On a waxing-moon evening, place the clear quartz crystal in front of the mirror.

2. Drizzle a drop of lavender oil on the crystal and another on the back of your hand to represent your desire to maintain, lose or gain weight.

3. On your piece of paper, write down the following affirmations:

> Food has no power over me.
>
> My self-respect and self-love are not dependent on the food I eat.
>
> I deserve to be exactly how I want to be.

4. Fold up the paper, wrap it around the crystal and place it under your pillow until the full moon.

5. On a full-moon evening, unfold your paper and repeat the three affirmations.

Having practised this ritual, you will be well on your way to consciously incorporating new strategies to keep your nutritional goals under control.

....

CHAMOMILE AND PEACH SMOOTHIE

★★
★

With its anti-spasmodic properties, chamomile is also used for calming the nervous and digestive systems and is an essential flower for supporting changeable Cancerian physical energy levels.

This nutritious smoothie will help to alleviate stress and is also a great way to start the day.

You will need:

* 1 chamomile tea bag (or make up some fresh chamomile flower tea and strain)
* ½ cup low-fat or non-dairy milk
* 1 peach, skinned and stoned
* 1 tsp grated fresh ginger

1. If using a tea bag, place it in a cup, cover with half a cup of boiling water and let it steep for about 5 minutes; if using a teapot and fresh flowers, let it steep for about 7 minutes.

2. When cool, place the strained tea in a blender with the remaining ingredients, blend until smooth and leave to chill for 20 minutes.

Honour the smoothie by making it a regular visitor at your breakfast table. You will enjoy feeling calm, yet energised and ready for the day ahead.

Beauty

Skincare and beauty routines can also be erratic for the Cancerian; yet with an uncanny sense of being at the right place at the right time, you're always there with the right make-up, the right hairstyle and flawless skin. Others may wonder how you manage to keep your complexion looking as pure as a moonstone, but little do they know that it's not just intuition, it's also a wise and resourceful knowledge of all the ancient techniques from the past. So continue to research traditional folk recipes, remedies, potions and powders to nurture the Crab's liking of traditional methods. By glamourising your outer beauty, the inner you will shine through, too.

....

DRAWING-DOWN-THE-MOON BATH

∗

Luxuriating in a sensuous, aromatic bath is one of Cancer's greatest pleasures. So here's a bath that adds the most nurturing of ingredients for skincare and body beautiful, while drawing down the power of the moon to nourish your inner beauty, too.

You will need:

* A moonstone
* 1 cup of almond oil
* A bottle with a lid (big enough to contain the moonstone)
* 5 drops of ylang-ylang essential oil
* 3 drops of sandalwood essential oil
* 2 drops of lavender essential oil
* 4 white tea lights

1. The morning before you take your bath, mix the oils in the bottle and add the moonstone. Shake gently and leave to infuse for at least the rest of the day (but it will keep for another week, if needed).

2. For your bath ritual, light the candles at the four corners of your bath, run the water and then slowly pour the prepared oil into the bath, holding back the moonstone.

3. Shake out the moonstone into your hand and place it at the end of your bath.

4. Sink into the joyful, calming water and, for a moment, reflect on the moonstone and its properties of self-healing, the beauty of moonlight, the power of its energy.

5. Next, take the moonstone and gently begin to massage it over your cheeks, making sure you do so with the flat surface. (You can use this moonstone massage as an overall body polish, too.)

This ritual will leave you feeling blessed with inner beauty and outer magic.

LEMONGRASS ESSENTIAL OIL CLEANSER

✳

Associated with the waning moon, lemongrass essential oil is one of the greatest detoxifying oils.

As Cancerians spend so much time tending to the needs of others, they come into contact with a lot of physical and psychic negativity. So to clear away emotional pollution from your auric field, dilute one drop of lemongrass oil in five parts of sweet almond oil and use daily as a morning or evening facial cleanser.

You can also dab a little oil on your finger and place on your third-eye chakra (see p. 95) every morning, to protect you from unwanted toxins, both environmental and psychic.

CHAKRA BALANCE

The body's chakras are the epicentres of the life-force energy that flows through all things (see p. 22).

Cancer is linked to the third-eye chakra, located in the centre of the forehead, between the eyebrows. The 'third eye' vibrates to the colours indigo and violet, and is concerned with inspiration, imagination and psychic ability.

When this chakra is underactive, you prevaricate more than usual, moodiness overwhelms you and you become defensive, retreating into your shell if you feel others don't understand you. You no longer trust your intuition and get clingy or possessive about other people. To restore balance and to feel centred and grounded, wear or carry amethyst (known for its empowering spiritual clarity). You will soon be 'in tune' with the universal energy, and everything will feel as if it's meant to be.

If this chakra is overactive, you live with your head in the clouds, your imagination working overtime, and spend a lot of time daydreaming. Wearing lapis lazuli (for concentration and self-knowledge) will help to subdue this chakra, so you can be more realistic, focused and confident in all you do.

General Wellbeing

For Cancer, the home is the place you love the most. Here, you can retreat from the world, indulge in fantastic dreams, wallow in your spiritual self, restore emotional strength and hide away if you just feel you don't want to see anyone. (And yes, caring about yourself means accepting that you *can* hide away and don't have to feel guilty about it!)

Here are some simple ways to maintain an overall sense of emotional and physical wellbeing by protecting and nurturing yourself and your home.

LUNAR CRYSTAL GRID
FOR PROTECTION

♡

The Cancerian home, embellished with beautiful things, is the proud statement of the perfect host, who has impeccable taste in food and comfortable surroundings. To make it even more restful and to protect you and your home from negative energy, place this lunar crystal grid by your front entrance.

You will need:
* 5 small pieces of selenite
* 5 small pieces of moonstone
* A large piece of black tourmaline
* Cypress essential oil
* A sage smudging stick

1. On the evening of a waxing moon, place the crystals spiralling out in an anticlockwise direction from the central black tourmaline, alternating selenite and moonstone.

2. Drizzle the cypress essential oil over each crystal.

3. Light your smudging stick and with it take a tour of your home. In each room or space, trace an imaginary circle in the air with the stick as you say: 'This lunar grid will protect myself and my family from all negativity'.

4. Return to the crystal grid and extinguish your sage stick. Leave the grid in place and, if you feel the need to reinforce this energy, repeat during a waxing-moon phase.

Left near your main entrance all year round, the grid will even remove negative psychic energy from visitors and keep your home stress-free.

HUG YOURSELF

♡

Behind that hard crab shell, you know you are a soft sensualist. That means you need to feel the emotional connection you have with the world, but also some tangible, physical sense of being part of it, too. So if you have a partner or loved one who can give you a hug every day – just for being you, not for anything more and with no expectations – you are off to a good start. It's the kind of closeness Cancerians need to truly feel loved and to be able to love themselves, too. Giving and receiving a hug is about not only embracing another person, but hugging the gift of life that is yourself.

If you don't have anyone to hug you right now, give yourself a big hug every day. Wrap your arms around yourself, whether naked or dressed up in your finery; it doesn't matter. All that's important is that you care for your physical presence, which deserves to be loved in the vast embrace of the Universe.

PART THREE

Caring For Your Soul

When you consider things like the stars, our affairs don't seem to matter very much, do they?

Virginia Woolf, English novelist

This final section offers you tailored, fun, easy and amazing ways to connect to and care for your sacred self. This, in turn, means you will begin to feel at one with the joyous energy of the Universe. You don't have to sign up to any religion or belief system (unless you want to) – just take some time to experience uplifting moments through your interaction with the spiritual aspects of the cosmos. Care for your sun sign's soul centre, and you care about the Universe, too.

Moon-ruled Cancer's sense of soul, or spirit, is informed by tried and trusted traditional ideas or beliefs. These connections give you a sense of belonging to some ancient or ancestral heritage. The Crab has a penchant for hoarding things – such as keepsakes, memories, souvenirs and old photos – so history, mythology and the ancient magical arts will nurture your soul. Because if what worked then works now, why change it for something new and risky? Most of all, Cancerians need to find a sacred cave or sanctuary deep within, and to draw inspiration from the mystery of themselves. This is why goddess religions, natural magic and other neopagan beliefs are perfect channels for spiritual care and are easily adapted to a sacred sanctuary in your home, where you can enjoy discovering your sacred self alone.

....

CONNECT TO THE ANCESTORS

✦✦
✦

The Crab's love of the past and their desire to know more about their family roots and lineage are good starting points for connecting to the spiritual world. Drawing on the beneficial energy of your ancestors means you can begin to feel guided and inspirited by those who have shaped part of your life.

You will need:

* A white candle
* A photograph of a favourite ancestor or family member who has passed* (or a copy, if you want to keep the original in a special place)
* A piece of black obsidian

* This doesn't have to be someone you have known personally – just someone whose features stand out from the crowd, who you've perhaps heard tales about or who achieved something you admire or respect in some way. They don't have to be recent ancestors either – they could be from several generations ago if you happened to have had your family tree drawn up (Cancerians do like delving into family archives).

1. On a full-moon night, light the candle and write your name on the back of the photo, along with these words: 'I bless you [their name] and thank you for connecting me to this spiritual home, where I will be protected and nourished by my ancestors'.

2. Place the obsidian on the photo, then focus for a moment on the candle flame to still your mind and open you to receiving their protection and a sense of sacred connection.

Keep the photo safe and repeat the ritual whenever you want to be spiritually blessed. Carry the obsidian with you as a homage to your ancestral heritage. Whenever you feel lost in your emotions or alone in the world, just turn the stone around and around in your hand, and you will find yourself again.

....

MAGIC LUNAR POUCH

✳

Aligned to the natural cycles of the moon and its influence on Earth, Cancerians want to believe the world is a magical place – and of course, it is, but belief starts within us, and one way to truly believe is to engage and align to Nature's powers.

Here's a way to get started with a moonstone, white rose and jasmine pouch, which will attract positive spiritual energy and healing into your life, while nurturing your Cancer soul.

You will need:
* 5 small moonstones
* A good handful of white rose petals
* A pouch
* A few drops of jasmine essential oil

1. In the evening of a waning or dark-of-the-moon phase, place the stones and rose petals in your pouch.

2. Gently shake the pouch, as you say the following: 'With lunar love, I bring to light my sacred secret self'.

3. Drizzle a few drops of jasmine oil on to the pouch to seal your intention for a magical connection to the Universe.

Place the pouch in a prominent position in your home where you will see it every day to affirm that you have found the magic of Nature within you, too.

MOON GLOW

♡

With Cancer's astrological affinity to the moon, use this simple symbolic lunar ritual to feel connected to your sacred self.

1. On a clear evening during a full moon, go outside if possible (to feel closer to the natural elements) and gaze up at the moon.

2. Make a circle with your finger and thumb, and hold it up to the sky, as if to surround the moon (adjust the size accordingly, starting at arm's length and then moving your hand towards you, until the moon 'fits' into your circle).

3. When you find the right position, say: 'My sacred self lies with the moon; she'll come to me and bring me spiritual joy whenever I hold her in this lunar ring'.

Whenever you would like some of the moon's spiritual guidance or comfort, simply raise your hand to the sky like this (whether the moon is visible or not) and gaze for a minute or so through your thumb-and-finger circle, imagining the glow of the moon, which will fill you with its mystical grace and power.

THE LABYRINTH VISUALISATION

★★
★

This is a simple visualisation practice to help you set the Crab's indecisive mind on track for spiritual growth. Whether you connect to the universal energy that flows through all things, feel at home with your ancestral spirit guide or are curious to find out more about Wicca, natural magic or Eastern philosophies, the labyrinth will help you to look more closely into what makes you feel spiritually enriched, and that will be the most precious channel to creative power and inner happiness.

1. Close your eyes and, with your finger stretched out before you, trace an imaginary labyrinth in the air. You don't know where it is going or where it will lead you, but just keep moving your finger to create your labyrinth, as if it were your spiritual guide. Keep going, spiralling, turning, imagining you are going deeper and deeper into the labyrinth, not worrying about having to go back – because when you have arrived you will know it; a feeling deep within.

2. Now visualise a signpost. Here, there is a choice of beliefs, of ways and means to lead you into the depths of your spiritual self. Stop moving your finger when you see the signpost and imagine the different destinations written on it, coming to you through your intuition. Whichever 'word' or image you see clearly will be the right pathway to follow.

3. Open your eyes, knowing the pathway unfolding before you.

4. Once you have tried this practice, it will no longer be up to you to choose the road because the road will have chosen you.

Last Words

If Cancerians weren't caring for others, then they wouldn't be living out their true potential. But the Crab also needs the emotional satisfaction that comes from looking after themselves. So this book reminds you to never forget to love yourself first and foremost. Once you begin to start to 'belong' to you (rather than to the demands, hopes, expectations and beliefs of others), and once you are your own puppeteer (rather than being strung up by your emotional need to be needed), you will wake up to the light of yourself and an authentic sense of self-containment.

With the help of astrological self-care, you should be starting to realise that it's your right to be not only the great homemaker, cook or carer, but also the mystic, the vamp or a nymph of the wild. There is a powerful creative impulse rooted in the depth and richness of Cancer's inner world. This can be channelled through caring for others of course, but also by living out all your other talents, whether your flair for the arts, your love of nature or your intuitive connection to the Universe. This creativity is generated from loving your unique Cancer self, and that astrological light that shines within. This inner light is mysterious and changeable and empowers you with great depth of wisdom, love for human nature and the empathy and knowledge of how people tick. Similarly, you can now begin to connect to this sacred self within, and, by touching this numinous centre, you touch the most beautiful, soulful part of you.

With this book you have begun to understand the watery world of the Crab, accept your emotional needs and express your personal desires. This book has shown you that it's ok to have feelings that fluctuate with changing energy – whether that of the moon or just your own inner rhythm. Yet there is more to Cancer than just caring for others – it's actually about the profound realisation that you have a generous and innate love to share. So it's time to share it with *you*, too, and to be uplifted by who you are becoming.

Resources

Main sites for crystals, stones, candles, smudging sticks, incense, pouches, essential oils and everything needed for the holistic self-care practices included in this book:

holisticshop.co.uk
thepsychictree.co.uk
thesoulangels.co.uk
earthcrystals.com
livrocks.com
artisanaromatics.com

For a substantial range of books (and metaphysical items) on astrology, divination, runes, palmistry, tarot and holistic health, etc.:

thelondonastrologyshop.com
watkinsbooks.com
mysteries.co.uk
barnesandnoble.com
innertraditions.com

For more information on astrology, personal horoscopes and birth-chart calculations:
astro-charts.com (simplest, very user friendly)

horoscopes.astro-seek.com
(straightforward)
astrolibrary.org/free-birth-chart
(easy to use, with lots of extra information)

Glossary

Aura An invisible electromagnetic energy field that emanates from and surrounds all living beings

Auric power The dominant colour of the aura that reveals your current mood or state

Chakra Sanskrit for 'wheel', in Eastern spiritual traditions the seven chakras are the main epicentres – or wheels – of invisible energy throughout the body

Dark of the moon This is when the moon is invisible to us, due to its proximity to the sun; it is a time for reflection, solitude and a deeper awareness of oneself

Divination Gaining insight into the past, present and future using symbolic or esoteric means

Double-terminator crystal A quartz crystal with a point at each end, allowing its energy to flow both ways

Full moon The sun is at its maximum opposition to the moon, thus casting light across all of the moon's orb; in esoteric terms, it is a time for culmination, finalising deals, committing to love and so on

Geopathic stress Negative energy emanating from and on the Earth, such as underground water courses, tunnels, overhead electrical cables and geological faults

Grid A specific pattern or layout of items symbolising specific intentions or desires

Horoscope An astrological chart or diagram showing the position of the sun, moon and planets at the time of any given event, such as the moment of somebody's birth, a marriage or the creation of an enterprise; it is used to interpret the characteristics or to forecast the future of that person or event

New crescent moon A fine sliver of crescent light that appears curving outwards to the right in the northern hemisphere and to the left in the southern hemisphere; this phase is for beginning new projects, new romance, ideas and so on

Psychic energy One's intuition, sixth sense or instincts, as well as the divine, numinous or magical power that flows through everything

Shadow side In astrology, your shadow side describes those aspects of your personality associated with your opposite sign and of which you are not usually aware

Smudging Clearing negative energy from the home with a smouldering bunch of dried herbs, such as sage

Solar return salutation A way to give thanks and welcome the sun's return to your zodiac sign once a year (your birthday month)

Sun in opposition The sun as it moves through the opposite sign to your own sun sign

Sun sign The zodiac sign through which the sun was moving at the exact moment of your birth

Waning moon The phase of the moon after it is full, when it begins to lose its luminosity – the waning moon is illuminated on its left side in the northern hemisphere, and on its right side in the southern hemisphere; this is a time for letting go, acceptance and preparing to start again

Waxing moon The phase between a new and a full moon, when it grows in luminosity – the waxing moon is illuminated on its right side in the northern hemisphere and on its left side in the southern hemisphere; this is a time for putting ideas and desires into practice

Zodiac The band of sky divided into twelve segments (known as the astrological signs), along which the paths of the sun, the moon and the planets appear to move

About the Author

After studying at the Faculty of Astrological Studies in London, the UK, Sarah gained the Diploma in Psychological Astrology – an in-depth 3-year professional training programme cross-fertilised by the fields of astrology and depth, humanistic and transpersonal psychology. She has worked extensively in the media as astrologer for titles such as *Cosmopolitan* magazine (UK), *SHE, Spirit & Destiny* and the *London Evening Standard*, and appeared on UK TV and radio shows, including *Steve Wright in the Afternoon* on BBC Radio 2.

Her mainstream mind-body-spirit books include the international bestsellers, *The Tarot Bible, The Little Book of Practical Magic* and *Secrets of the Universe in 100 Symbols*.

Sarah currently practises and teaches astrology and other esoteric arts in the heart of the countryside.

Acknowledgements

I would first like to thank everyone at Yellow Kite, Hodder & Stoughton and Hachette UK who were part of the process of creating this series of twelve zodiac self-care books. I am especially grateful to Carolyn Thorne for the opportunity to write these guides; Anne Newman for her editorial advice, which kept me 'carefully' on the right track; and Olivia Nightingall who kept me on target for everything else! It is when people come together with their different skills and talents that the best books are made – so I am truly grateful for being part of this team.

See the full Astrology Self-Care series here

9781399704885   9781399704915   9781399704588

9781399704618   9781399704649   9781399704670

9781399704700   9781399704731   9781399704762

9781399704793   9781399704823   9781399704854

yellow
kite

books to help you live a good life

Join the conversation and tell
us how you live a #goodlife

@yellowkitebooks
YellowKiteBooks
Yellow Kite Books
YellowKiteBooks